Original title:

Ebon Halts Among the Griffin Yoke

Copyright © 2025 Swan Charm

All rights reserved.

Author: Aron Pilviste

ISBN HARDBACK: 978-1-80563-221-4

ISBN PAPERBACK: 978-1-80564-742-3

Beneath the Twilight Canopy

Beneath the twilight, shadows creep,
Whispers flutter, secrets deep.
Stars awaken, one by one,
In the embrace of day's undone.

Moonbeams dance on silver streams,
Casting light on midnight dreams.
Through the leaves, a soft refrain,
Echoes of a forgotten name.

Creatures stir in dusky air,
Wings spread wide, a gentle flair.
In this realm, the magic flows,
A tapestry the twilight sews.

Candles flicker in the gloom,
Carving out a sacred room.
Hearts entwined and souls laid bare,
In this stillness, nothing's rare.

As dreams take flight on velvet night,
Hope ignites in shimmering light.
Beneath the canopy, we find,
A world that beckons, unexplined.

Bonds Affixed in Celestial Twilight

In twilight's weave, a tale is spun,
Of bonds forged where time's begun.
Stars entwined in endless arcs,
Igniting hearts with cosmic sparks.

Constellations hang like dreams,
Among soft sighs and silvery beams.
Whispers brush our cheeks like fate,
As we gather, hearts elate.

Light and shadow dance in play,
Bringing forth the dusk of day.
Each moment swells, a breath of peace,
In night's embrace, our worries cease.

With every pulse, the night unfolds,
A tapestry of tales retold.
Each star reflects a path anew,
A promise made, a dream in view.

Through the silence, echoes call,
In twilight's thrall, we rise, we fall.
Beneath the vast celestial dome,
We find in shadows, a way back home.

A Ritual of Shadows and Grasped Dreams

Gather round, as shadows weave,
A ritual to dare, believe.
In the circle, candles glint,
Whispers carry what we imprint.

Hands joined tight, hearts in sync,
Time suspends, we pause, we think.
Adrift in waves of twilight's hue,
Our wishes take flight, bold and true.

Secrets twine through branches bare,
Casting thoughts into the air.
With every word, our hopes arise,
A symphony beneath the skies.

The night hums low, a haunting song,
Guiding spirits, where they belong.
In shadows deep, we grasp our dreams,
In unity, the magic gleams.

As moonlight spills, we dare to chase,
What dwells beneath the world's face.
With painted skies, our dreams take flight,
In shadows' dance, we claim the night.

Bondage of Talon and Heart

In shadows deep, where echoes dwell,
A tale unfolds, of charm and spell.
A talon strong, a heart so true,
Together bound, in skies so blue.

Their whispers weave, a magic rare,
In every glance, a secret shared.
Through trials fierce, their spirits soar,
In love's embrace, they seek for more.

The darkness calls, with tempting waltz,
Yet courage blooms, when hope exalts.
With each embrace, they forge ahead,
Through storm and strife, where few dare tread.

The world may twist, its cruel design,
But hand in hand, their stars align.
From ash and fire, their bond takes flight,
Through endless realms, both day and night.

In twilight's glow, their shadows blend,
The journey grand, with no clear end.
In every beat, their hearts proclaim,
The talon's grip, the heart's pure flame.

Chronicles of the Cursed Sky

Beneath the veil of stormy dread,
A chronicle, where few have tread.
The cursed sky, a haunting sight,
In whispered tales, lost to the night.

Winds of fate, they twist and whirl,
A tapestry where secrets unfurl.
With weary eyes, the brave take flight,
In search of truths, shrouded in light.

Each cloud a memory, lost in time,
A haunting echo, a silent chime.
The stars align in cryptic dance,
Yet shadows linger, in fate's romance.

On broken wings, the lost take heed,
With hearts aflame, they dare proceed.
In battles fought, their spirits rise,
Against the backdrop of cursed skies.

Though darkness whispers, and fear may strive,
With courage bold, they come alive.
Each chapter penned, a legacy spun,
In the cursed sky, where hopes are won.

Veils of Shade Across Ancient Peaks

In ancient lands, where shadows play,
The veils of shade mark the pathway.
With whispered thoughts and secrets old,
The mountains guard their tales of gold.

In twilight hours, the breezes sigh,
Among the peaks that kiss the sky.
With every step, a mystery stirs,
Where earth and sky, the spirit blurs.

The echoes dance in crisp, cool air,
With every glance, a world laid bare.
The veils once drawn, now drift away,
Revealing truths in soft array.

Through hidden paths and rugged stone,
A journey made, yet not alone.
For in the depths, their spirits rise,
As shadows lean beneath the skies.

With lessons penned in each old stone,
In every breath, wisdom's own.
The veils of shade tell tales profound,
In ancient peaks, where dreams are found.

Guardians of the Gloom's Embrace

In twilight's glow, the silence falls,
To muted cries, as darkness calls.
Guardians stand, both brave and bold,
They shield the secrets, never told.

With watchful eyes, they guard the night,
When shadows stretch beyond the light.
In solemn oaths, they make their vow,
To keep the realms safe, here and now.

Amongst the gloom, their strength shines bright,
A beacon fierce, in endless night.
Each whispered word, a magic spun,
In every heart, the fight's begun.

When fear encroaches, their spirits soar,
Through trials faced, forevermore.
With hands entwined, they forge their fate,
As guardians stand, and hope awaits.

In the realm of dusk, where shadows reside,
They face the storm, the turning tide.
For in their hearts, a flame remains,
The guardians of the gloom's domains.

Emblems of Gloom in Avian Majesty

In shadows cast by ancient trees,
The crows declare their mournful pleas.
With wings spread wide, they take to flight,
Emblems of gloom in fading light.

Through whispers of the darkest night,
They dance and dive, a haunting sight.
In every flap, the secrets keep,
Of dreams that wake, of dreams that sleep.

Their calls resound like thunder's roar,
Echoing tales of times before.
Against the dusk, their forms entwine,
In twilight's grasp, a fate divine.

With every beat, a story shared,
Of sorrows borne, of hearts laid bare.
In realms of twilight's waning hue,
These avian souls, forever true.

So heed the sky, where shadows dwell,
For in their flight, the lost can tell.
Of love, of loss, of yearning deep,
Emblems of gloom their secrets keep.

Flight Toward the Abyss of Time

When twilight gathers, dreams take wing,
To chase the echoes, time's own sting.
In spirals vast, they twist and turn,
Toward the abyss, where shadows yearn.

The winds of ages whisper low,
Guiding the hearts that dare to go.
With every crack, the past ignites,
In flights toward unknown nights.

From heights unknown, they see below,
Where hours drift like autumn's snow.
Each moment weighed, each second lost,
In search of warmth, despite the frost.

As clocks unwind and stars collide,
In cosmic dance, no place to hide.
The universe, a silent rhyme,
Calling forth the wings of time.

So soar with grace, to realms sublime,
For in the flight, we conquer time.
Amidst the night, with heart so bold,
Our stories weave, our truths unfold.

The Weight of Wings in Stillness

Beneath the hush, the world holds breath,
Where silence reigns, and whispers death.
The weight of wings, in stillness lies,
As shadows dance 'neath leaden skies.

Yet in the dark, the heartbeats swell,
A tale unfolds, a muted spell.
Each feather draped in dreams anew,
In stillness, life can pierce right through.

The echoes of forgotten song,
Beneath the calm, the pulse grows strong.
In every twitch, a spark ignites,
As night retreats for dawn's delights.

With every beat, the power flows,
In solemn grace, the silence grows.
The weight of wings, a pledge of flight,
A promise borne on golden light.

So cherish stillness, heed the call,
For in its depths, we rise or fall.
The weight of dreams, the strength we crave,
In quiet moments, we become brave.

Serpentines of Darkened Skies

In serpentines of darkened skies,
The night unfolds its silent cries.
With twisting trails, the shadows roam,
In cosmic dance, they seek their home.

Each flicker, glint, a fleeting spark,
In depths where daylight fears to hark.
They spiral high, on whispers rise,
In the embrace of starry lies.

Past echoes haunt, as dreams entwine,
A tapestry of fate divine.
With every turn, the mysteries spun,
In swirling grace, the threads come undone.

The darkness weaves a tale so bright,
In serpentines of whispered light.
Where shadows breathe and spirits play,
A world reborn, anew each day.

So linger here, in twilight's glow,
Embrace the night, let your heart flow.
For in the dance of darkened skies,
We find our truth, we learn to rise.

Bound by Celestial Chains

In the realm where shadows dwell,
Stars whisper tales, cast their spell.
Celestial chains, a binding grace,
Hold our fates in time and space.

Winds of fate, they bend and sway,
Guiding spirits on their way.
In the night, we weave our dreams,
Through the starlight's gentle beams.

Moonlight dances on the ground,
Echoes of a past profound.
Beneath the watchful, ancient skies,
Our hearts united, never die.

In the silence, secrets bloom,
Painted vividly, dispel the gloom.
Chains of stardust, bright and tight,
Guide us through the darkest night.

Together born, forever linked,
In this tapestry, we're distinct.
Gathering strength from worlds unknown,
Bound by chains, but never alone.

When the Wind Carries Secrets

When the wind carries secrets low,
Whispers of the past in tow.
Leaves will dance on twilight's breath,
As they weave the tales of death.

Softly they swirl, like dreams untold,
A story of the brave and bold.
In the rustling trees, they reside,
Echoes of those who once were tried.

The chill of night, a canvas dark,
Where shadows flicker, leaving marks.
Muffled laughter, distant cries,
Carried far beneath the skies.

Secrets borne on whispers light,
Symphonies of day and night.
In the gust, a fleeting chance,
To remember, to dream, to dance.

For every gust speaks of our fate,
Unraveling threads, it won't wait.
Listen close, for you shall see,
What the night wishes to be free.

The Keeper of the Unworn Path

In twilight's grace, the path is drawn,
Beneath the watchful gaze of dawn.
A keeper waits, with wisdom grand,
To guide the lost through shadowed land.

With steps so light, the journey starts,
Tracing lines of ancient hearts.
Each stone a memory, softly laid,
A tapestry of light and shade.

The air is thick with dreams once spun,
Stories lost, yet never done.
Time stands still in this embrace,
The keeper smiles, in quiet grace.

Through verdant woods and skies so wide,
The unworn path, where dreams abide.
With every turn, a chance to find,
The solace of the heart entwined.

So step forth bold, with open eyes,
For in the unseen, true magic lies.
The keeper's call is ever near,
On this path, you have no fear.

Starlit Bonds of Myth and Memory

In the secret glades where starlight glows,
Myths are kept, where memory flows.
Stories twirl on silken threads,
Binding hearts where destiny spreads.

Underneath the vast expanse,
Each twinkling star has found its chance.
To weave the tales of yesterdays,
In shimmering hues, like the sun's rays.

Whispers of ancients, soft and clear,
Echo through time, the past draws near.
In every tale, a truth unfolds,
In starlit bonds, our fate is told.

Time bends here, like a silver stream,
Carrying our hopes, our dreams to gleam.
With every heartbeat, the ties grow strong,
Myth and memory, where we belong.

So gather round, and share the light,
In celestial dance, our spirits bright.
Together we weave, we sing, we soar,
In starlit bonds, forevermore.

Tales between the Beast and the Night

In twilight's grasp where shadows creep,
A whisper echoes, secrets keep.
Beneath the stars, the beasts allure,
Guardians of the night, so pure.

With eyes that gleam like fiery coals,
They weave the stories of lost souls.
Through tangled woods, their voices sing,
Of ancient times and what they bring.

The moon, a watchful, silver eye,
Sees all the wonders racing by.
Creatures dance in silent grace,
They mirror dreams and time's embrace.

From shadows deep, new legends rise,
Beneath the skies where magic lies.
Each tale, a thread in fate's fine loom,
Weaving light within the gloom.

So listen close as night unfolds,
The tales of courage, brave and bold.
For every beast, both fierce and bright,
Is just a story clad in night.

Chains of the Winged Keeper

In a tower high, where echoes wail,
Lies a keeper, bound by fate's frail trail.
With wings of silver, faith worn thin,
He guards the realms where dreams begin.

Each morning breaks with chains anew,
The weight of worlds he must pursue.
He longs to soar beyond the cell,
To break the spell and tolling bell.

Through crystal skies and azure streams,
He fights the shadows, chases dreams.
Yet in his heart, a flicker glows,
Of hope that only freedom knows.

With every gust, the air must sing,
He yearns to feel the joy of spring.
A whispered promise, sworn in breath,
That chains will fade, and flee from death.

The winds call out with beckoning hands,
To break the shackles of distant lands.
As twilight falls, he sings his plight,
The chains may bind, but not the night.

Beneath the Gaze of the Shadowed Sphinx

In deserts wide where secrets blend,
A Sphinx sits still, her gaze can bend.
She holds the truths of ages lost,
In riddles deep, at a heavy cost.

Her eyes reflect the moonlit sands,
As travelers seek her silent commands.
With caution shared in every breath,
They ponder all the ties of death.

Each question asked, a step in dark,
The answers shroud the hidden spark.
With patience grand, she shares her lore,
But only those who seek can score.

Underneath her patient gaze,
The secrets swirl in mystic haze.
For wisdom guards a fragile key,
Unlocking doors to the unseen sea.

Yet daring hearts must take the chance,
To tread the line, to join the dance.
For doubted thoughts may give you flight,
Beneath the gaze of Sphinx at night.

The Last Flight of the Celestial Bound

On wings of dusk, they soar and glide,
The cosmic whispers swell with pride.
In argent trails where dreams collide,
The celestial bound, their fates reside.

With glimmers bright against the dark,
They trace the paths, leave trails of spark.
In quiet grace, the heavens sing,
A chorus of the night they bring.

Yet time it seems, begins to fray,
As stars twinkle with a fading ray.
The last flight calls, a bittersweet,
To weave their tales of joy complete.

Across the sky, their stories weep,
As constellations begin to sleep.
Through twilight's breath, they gladly dive,
In memories, their spirits thrive.

So when you gaze at night's embrace,
Remember well their fleeting grace.
For in the silence, their truth resounds,
The last flight of the celestial bounds.

The Covenant of Two Realms

In twilight's breath, the pact was sealed,
A whisper soft, the fates revealed.
Two realms entwined, a bond so true,
With shadows cast, the light breaks through.

The forest hums with ancient lore,
While rivers sing of those before.
Two worlds collide beneath the stars,
In unity, they'll conquer scars.

A silver thread weaves through the night,
Guiding souls as spirits take flight.
In every heart, a sign will show,
The covenant that ever grows.

Tales Woven in the Shade of Greatness

In the hush of night, where dreams take form,
Legends slumber, safe from the storm.
With ink and quill, the stories weave,
In shadows cast, where we believe.

The echoes of laughter fill the air,
With each soft sigh, a magic rare.
Heroes rise and fall like leaves,
In silent woods, where hope believes.

Beneath the boughs, the whispers tell,
Of distant lands where spirits dwell.
In every heart, a tale unfolds,
Woven in shades of red and gold.

When Storms Call the Winged Beings

When thunder rolls through skies of gray,
The winged beings come out to play.
With flaps of silk, they dance and glide,
Bringing forth the tempest's pride.

Clouds collide in a vibrant fray,
As lightning strikes, they find their way.
In swirling winds, their voices rise,
A lullaby to stormy skies.

With feathers bright, they'll soar and dive,
In nature's heart, they'll feel alive.
When calm returns, they take to rest,
In dreams of storms, they are the best.

The Pact Between Earth and Sky

Beneath the stars, a promise made,
Where earth and sky in silence played.
Roots entwined with celestial grace,
In harmony, they found their place.

The mountains rise to kiss the clouds,
In ancient air, their spirits loud.
Each drop of rain, a whispered vow,
To nurture life in here and now.

The sunset paints the world anew,
As day surrenders, shadows grew.
In twilight's hush, the pact will shine,
A bond eternal, pure and divine.

Tribulations Born from Feathered Lyres

In twilight's glow where shadows play,
Feathered tunes weave tales of gray.
Whispers echo through the trees,
Soft as whispers, carried by breeze.

A melody lost in sorrow's sigh,
Laments of braves who dared to fly.
Each note a memory, each chord a tear,
In the hush of dusk, their voices near.

Through trials vast and tempests wild,
The lyres of fate, both cruel and mild.
With every pluck, a story told,
Of love and loss, of hearts so bold.

Time's tender hand, it shall not cease,
In melodies, we find our peace.
For every feathered note we strum,
A promise kept, though fate may come.

So heed the calls that echo long,
In feathered lyres, we find our song.
Let tribulations guide our way,
In harmony, we find our stay.

The Constellation's Oath

Stars are scattered like dreams untold,
In the canvas of night, their glimmers bold.
They whisper secrets to the waking world,
An oath at twilight, unfurled.

Each twinkle a promise, each sparkle a vow,
To guard the slumbering earth below.
With ancient grace, they watch and shine,
In the cloaks of night, their fates align.

Galaxies dance in celestial waltz,
While time drips slowly, it never halts.
Constellations weave stories bright,
Of love and longing, in the night.

Through ages past, they've stood the test,
A guiding light, a soothing jest.
In stardust dreams and silvered beams,
We find our hopes, we find our themes.

Upon a night when wishes fade,
The stars shall bind the oaths they made.
With every heartbeat and every sigh,
The constellations sing their reply.

Threads of Fate in Winged Soliloquy

In the quietude of dawn's soft light,
Threads of fate weave tales in flight.
Winged whispers twirl in the breeze,
Carrying thoughts on daybreak's tease.

Gossamer strands of hopes and dreams,
Flutter like leaves in sunlit beams.
Each thread a journey, bold and bright,
A tapestry spun in morning's light.

Soliloquy sung by feathered kin,
Of journeys far where dreams begin.
Through valleys deep and mountains high,
On wings of wishes, they soar and fly.

A dance of fate, a fleeting glance,
In the heart's weave, they take their chance.
The chorus of wings, a song so sweet,
In the quiet dawn, their hearts compete.

So let the threads in daylight's grip,
Guide every dream and imagined trip.
For in the woven tapestry's folds,
We find the strength that life beholds.

The Allegiance of Beasts at Twilight

Beneath the cloak of evening's glow,
The beasts of the wild gather slow.
In shadows deep where secrets lie,
They pledge their oaths beneath the sky.

The howl of the wolf, the flutter of wings,
In unity, the forest sings.
Together they stand, a noble band,
Guardians fierce of their enchanted land.

As twilight whispers, the pact is made,
Through thickets dense and glades that fade.
Each creature bound by honor's call,
In the heart of the wood, they rise or fall.

With every hoofbeat and echoing roar,
They share the bonds that they adore.
From the mightiest bears to the smallest hare,
In allegiance sworn, they stand and stare.

Upon this night, when shadows blend,
They find a strength that will not bend.
The creatures of night, in unity thrive,
For in their hearts, they keep hope alive.

Thus echo the vows in twilight's embrace,
In the kingdom of dusk, they find their place.
The allegiance of beasts, a timeless song,
In harmony, they forever belong.

Shadowed Stirrings of the Winged Beast

In whispered woods where shadows dwell,
A creature stirs its silent spell,
With crimson eyes that pierce the night,
It takes to air, a fleeting sight.

From ancient roots, the legends soar,
Of mystic wings and tales of yore,
Through silver mist, it sweeps its grace,
In twilight's fold, it finds its place.

The wind now carries echoes bold,
Of whispered dreams and stories told,
Its feathered form, a fleeting glance,
Of magic born from night's romance.

Beneath the stars, the shadows play,
In midnight's glow, the skies hold sway,
With every flap, the heartbeats race,
A dance of fate, the wild embrace.

Awakened fears, yet hope shall bloom,
In darkness deep, dispelling gloom,
For in the night, the beast takes flight,
A shadowed stir of pure delight.

A Midnight Pact Beneath Feathers

Beneath the arch of ancient trees,
A pact is made upon the breeze,
With whispered words that twine and swell,
The secrets weave a hidden spell.

In shimmering cloaks of midnight hue,
The winged convene, both brave and true,
With every heartbeat, fate's design,
An oath of trust, their spirits bind.

With feathered quills and dreams in tow,
They fly to realms where wonders grow,
Through midnight realms, the essence glows,
A thread of stars, the silence knows.

They speak of hope, and brave anew,
As dawn approaches, the sky in blue,
In feathered flight, they find their song,
A melody to which they belong.

And as the sun breaks night's cruel hold,
Their pact remains, a bond of gold,
In every flap, a promise true,
For midnight's pact, forever due.

The Silent Sorrow of Dusk Wings

Once in the hush of twilight's fade,
A silent sorrow begins to wade,
For creatures lost in shadows' veil,
Their stories woven, soft as a trail.

The dusk it brings a weeping sigh,
As memories swirl and gently lie,
With every flap, a fleeting grace,
They search the skies for a warm embrace.

In muted flight, their whispers blend,
Through twilight's haze, where wraiths descend,
Once proud and free, now bound to roam,
The dusk wings call, a yearning home.

Yet in their hearts, a light still gleams,
A spark that threads through broken dreams,
They chase the stars, their souls alight,
In sorrow's grip, they find their flight.

So listen close as night unfolds,
The silent tales of hearts so bold,
For in the air, their essence sings,
A haunting tune of dusk's lost wings.

Echoes of a Tethered Dream

In realms where echoes softly dwell,
A tethered dream begins to swell,
With every pulse, the visions fly,
Through silken threads that weave the sky.

They whisper secrets, shared in flight,
Beneath the stars, in endless night,
The heartbeats pulse, a rhythmic song,
To follow dreams, where we belong.

With every gust, the whispers sway,
A symphony of night and day,
The threads of hope, a binding seam,
A dance of life, an endless dream.

From feathered wings, the shadows cast,
In every flicker, futures vast,
Yet every tether holds it tight,
As echoes blend with fading light.

With open hearts, the night shall bend,
To cradle dreams, no need to end,
For in the silence, voices rise,
In echoes shared, through boundless skies.

The Veil of Secrets in Each Feather

In shadows deep where whispers play,
Each feather holds a tale's array.
Secrets wrapped in silken thread,
Where dreams take flight and fears are shed.

Beneath the moon's soft, watchful gaze,
They dance and shine in twilight's haze.
With every rustle, ancient sighs,
Unfold as stars in midnight skies.

In forests lush, where spirits tread,
The echoes of the lost are fed.
They flutter close, a gentle breeze,
Entrancing hearts that dare to seize.

Across the lands, in whispers small,
The secrets beckon, one and all.
Unlock the thoughts on plumage spun,
Reveal the mysteries, one by one.

So listen well to the feather's song,
For within its folds, you'll find where you belong.
Embrace the tales that softly flow,
The veil of secrets, watch them grow.

The Roar of Dusk's Consort

When shadows blend and day retreats,
A symphony of night repeats.
The roar of dusk, a wild embrace,
Awakening stars, a radiant race.

The winds will carry secrets bold,
Of ancient tales and stories told.
Guided by the moon's soft sway,
The night reveals its grand ballet.

In hidden glades, where darklings roam,
The call of twilight, a heart's true home.
With every whisper, every sigh,
The dusk's consort bids day goodbye.

Amongst the trees, the spirits weave,
A tapestry we dare believe.
In every rustle, every sound,
The echoes of vast realms abound.

So heed the roar beneath the skies,
Where night and day, their dance comprises.
For in the twilight's glowing mist,
Lies a world that can't be missed.

Echoes of Legends That Bind

In whispered dreams where legends dwell,
The echoes weave a timeless spell.
A tapestry of fate and choice,
Where ancient hearts can still rejoice.

Through winding paths and hallowed halls,
The voice of history gently calls.
A melody both fierce and sweet,
Resounding rhythms, a wondrous beat.

For every name that's carved in stone,
An echo's truth is surely sown.
With each step forth, the fabric bends,
Uniting souls, where lineage blends.

In twilight's hush, the stories merge,
Of courage fierce and love's great surge.
Their binding force shall never wane,
Through joy and sorrow, bliss and pain.

So let us gather 'round the fire,
Where echoes lift our hearts up higher.
As legends live and shadows fade,
We find our strength; we're not afraid.

Breach of the Aether's Veil

In realms unseen where spirits dwell,
The breach of aether's shining shell.
Whispers ride on zephyrs' wings,
Unraveling the truth that sings.

Through cosmic threads, in vibrant hues,
The hidden worlds begin to fuse.
With every breath, a dream takes flight,
Illuminating the endless night.

Where stars align and fortunes weave,
A tapestry of all who believe.
In twilight's glow, the veil is torn,
Revealing wonders, new and worn.

Echoes shimmer, calling forth,
The lost, the loved, a soulful worth.
Journey forth through time and space,
Embrace the whispers, find your place.

As dawn approaches, shadows flee,
The aether's breath empowers thee.
So dare to venture, hearts unveiled,
For in this breach, a truth is hailed.

Enigmas of the Nightbound Gale

In shadows deep where secrets sleep,
the whispering winds of twilight creep.
Moonlit paths where echoes dwell,
tales untold weave a magic spell.

Stars alight in a velvet sky,
dancing dreams as the hours fly.
Olden trees with branches wide,
guard the mysteries that they hide.

Crickets sing in the still of night,
a chorus soft, a soothing light.
Beneath the veil, the world turns slow,
as twilight paints the earth below.

Glimmers spark where shadows loom,
shapes of night in the silent gloom.
Whispers trace the edges of fate,
each promise whispered, never late.

For in the dark, all secrets find,
the language spoken by the blind.
The nightbound gale knows every tale,
as galaxies spin, and dreams unveil.

Whispers in the Roost of Twilight

In twilight's arms, where shadows play,
the softest whispers drift away.
Nestled still in the fading light,
where day surrenders to the night.

Feathers rustle in gentle grace,
moon-bright eyes hold a hidden place.
Secrets float on a silken breeze,
wrapped in twilight's tender tease.

Crimson hues fade to shades of grey,
dancing lightly as night holds sway.
Lore of ages in silence weaves,
cloaked in the comfort that twilight leaves.

Hushed are the cries of the weary owls,
and soft are the hoofprints of roaming fowls.
The roost hums low, a lullaby,
where dreams are sown and whispers fly.

Within this realm, the unknown stirs,
an echo born where magic purrs.
Beneath the stars, the heart knows how,
to breathe the wonder of the now.

The Last Flight of the Shrouded Guardian

Through midnight's veil on wings so wide,
the guardian soars, a stormy tide.
Wrapped in shadows, cloaked in might,
a watchful soul in the deep of night.

With each beat, the heavens tremble,
as ancient secrets start to assemble.
Skyward dreams in a daring flight,
chasing the dawn, embracing the light.

Beneath the stars, stories entwine,
as fate doth weave its whispered line.
In every gust, a tale reborn,
in the heart of night, a spirit worn.

The shrouded guardian, bold and wise,
imprisoned dreams to the endless skies.
With feathers dark as the void unfurled,
it carries the hopes of the waking world.

And when the dawn with petals blush,
it sings of a past where shadows rush.
One last flight, a final call,
as sunlight breaks and shrouds all.

Secrets Weaved in Silver Feathers

In the quiet hush of the starry night,
a tapestry spun in silvery light.
With whispers soft like a lover's sigh,
secrets deep in the feathered sky.

Glimmers fall where the moonlight glows,
casting spells in the night that flows.
Each strand woven with delicate care,
a story held in the silver air.

Owls take flight on wings of grace,
through shadowed paths, they find their place.
Mysteries linger in the cool night breeze,
woven like dreams in the rustling leaves.

A shiver of stars, the night unfolds,
ancient tales that the evening holds.
Each feather's plight, a whispered call,
that dances lightly, inspiring all.

In the heart of night, where silence roams,
the secrets weave and the wanderer roams.
Bound by whispers, the stories rise,
in silver feathers beneath the skies.

In the Hold of Winged Nightmares

In shadows deep where fears reside,
The hollow calls of night abide.
With lurking whispers weaving dread,
The winged nightmares dance ahead.

They soar beneath a cloak of gloom,
Each flap a harbinger of doom.
In moonlit trails, for souls to claim,
They bring forth sorrow, doubt, and shame.

A trembling heart in silence screams,
While phantoms twist the waking dreams.
These haunting forms, both fierce and sly,
They linger as the stars burn high.

Yet in the darkness, courage grows,
For in the night, true magic flows.
With wand in hand, let spirits rise,
Against the feasting of the skies.

For every shadow holds a light,
A spark to pierce the veil of night.
In battles fought, and lessons learned,
The flame of hope forever burned.

Threads of Fate in Feathered Darkness

In fields where whispered secrets lay,
The fates entwine through night and day.
With feathers spun from dreams and sighs,
They weave the tales where laughter dies.

Each thread a story, finely drawn,
In twilight's grip before the dawn.
They flutter softly, shimmering bright,
A tapestry of dark and light.

Yet as the loom begins to twist,
A shadow creeps, a haunting mist.
In every stitch of sorrowed fate,
A longing souls can hardly sate.

But brave are those who dare to tread,
Through paths where whispers have been led.
With every tear and dropped embrace,
They stitch anew the fractured space.

For life's a dance, both brave and bold,
In shadows deep, true hearts are sold.
To weave, to mend, to fly once more,
Through threads of fate, our spirits soar.

The Flight You Never Flew

Beneath the stars, you dreamed of flight,
In whispered winds that kiss the night.
Yet chains of doubt held fast your heart,
From skies unknown, you drifted far apart.

Each wish a bird, in shadows caged,
With every longing, fears engaged.
The winds would call; you'd hear them sing,
Yet tethered still, you felt no wing.

But what if courage found its way,
To pierce the veil of darker day?
In every breath, a spark ignites,
The path of dreams unfolds in sights.

With wings of light, you'd break the spell,
To soar beyond the shadows' hell.
Through clouds of doubt, your spirit flies,
Embracing all the endless skies.

For every heart can learn to soar,
If only we could ask for more.
To take the flight, to rise anew,
And chase the dreams we never flew.

Terrors in the Plume of Starlit Rebellion

In the quiet nights where shadows dwell,
A whisper stirs, an ancient spell.
The rebels rise with fire in eyes,
While starlit dreams begin to vaporize.

With feathers black and hearts aflame,
They gather strength, they seek a name.
For every flutter, every cry,
Is etched upon the midnight sky.

Yet terrors lurk in every flight,
In mindful hearts, the hope ignites.
For every tale of war's embrace,
Shines light upon a starry face.

As battles loom, the winds will change,
The rebel spirits rearrange.
In twilight's grasp, are truths revealed,
The power held, the magic sealed.

So rise, ye souls, and take your stand,
In plume of starlight, take command.
For in rebellion's fiercest gleam,
Lies the power to fulfill a dream.

The Silent Bond of Mythical Kin

In shadows deep where whispers blend,
A kinship forged that will not bend.
With eyes aglow like stars on high,
Their hearts in silence dare not lie.

Among the woods where secrets creep,
The bonds of lore in silence seep.
Together they, both fierce and true,
In hidden realms they weave anew.

The moonlight casts a silver thread,
A tapestry of words unsaid.
In mythic halls where echoes hum,
Together, still, they shall become.

Through ages past and futures bright,
Their spirits soar like birds in flight.
Across the veil of time they roam,
The silent bond shall lead them home.

In every tale of woe or grace,
Their presence weaves a magic space.
And though the world may turn and spin,
The strength of kin lies deep within.

Reverie Beneath the Glistening Wing

Beneath the arch of glistening flight,
Dreams unfurl in endless night.
As shadows dance in silver glow,
A reverie where secrets flow.

With feathers soft as whispered dreams,
The winged ones weave enchanted seams.
They guide the hearts that dare to seek,
With tender grace, they softly speak.

In twilight's hush, where magic stirs,
Their silent song through air confers.
A realm where hopes like feathers drift,
In realms of light, the shadows lift.

Beneath each wing a tale resides,
Of journeys vast and hidden tides.
With every flutter, dreams take flight,
In reverie, hearts find their light.

So close your eyes, embrace the sky,
Where glistening wings will never die.
In every heart their echoes sing,
A world reborn through glistening wing.

Portents in the Lair of Legends

In caverns deep where shadows dwell,
The ancient lore begins to swell.
With whispered breath and secrets old,
Portents rise, their tales unfold.

The dragon's roar, a thrilling sign,
Echoing through the sacred line.
Beneath the stone, the legends weave,
A tapestry that none believe.

In flickers bright of molten glow,
They guide the seekers through the throe.
With every turn of time and fate,
The tales of yore, forever great.

A clash of swords, a heart ablaze,
Within the lair, a fiery maze.
In every beat, a story spins,
The echoes swell where legend begins.

Through darkness thick where shadows play,
The portents lift, they light the way.
In every heart, a spark of fire,
In the lair of legends, dreams aspire.

Dreams Awakened Under Hidden Wings

In twilight's shroud where dreams reside,
Awakened hearts in silence bide.
With hidden wings that softly sway,
In shadows deep, they find their way.

A gentle breeze that stirs the night,
Whispers secrets, soft and bright.
Beneath the stars, the world anew,
Awakens hope, the sky's own hue.

Through tangled roots and silver streams,
Their presence glows within our dreams.
In twilight's glow, they weave their song,
A melody where we belong.

As wings unfurl, they sweep us high,
To realms where thoughts like shadows fly.
In every heart, their magic sings,
Awakening the strength that clings.

Upon the dawn, with light in hand,
We rise anew, we take our stand.
With hidden wings, our spirits soar,
In dreams awakened, we explore.

Beneath Canopies of Winged Wisdom

In woodland whispers, secrets dwell,
Where moonlit creatures weave their spell.
Beneath the canopies, wisdom flies,
A tapestry woven through starlit skies.

With wings aflutter, truths alight,
In shadows where the day meets night.
Old souls whisper in the breeze,
Teaching hearts with gentle ease.

The forest sighs, a lullaby,
Each rustling leaf a soft goodbye.
Among the branches, visions bloom,
Awakening dreams from velvet gloom.

In every flutter, secrets yearn,
For those who seek, the world does turn.
The wisdom found in quiet grace,
Guides the seeker to their place.

So linger long, let time unspool,
In nature's arms, be still, be cool.
For in the silence, magic dwells,
Beneath the canopies, wisdom swells.

The Grasp of the Luminous Grip

In the dawn's embrace, light takes flight,
Fingers of gold spark at night.
The luminous grip holds all in thrall,
A radiant touch that enchants all.

With each golden ray, secrets unfold,
Whispers of stories waiting to be told.
Embraced by warmth, hearts ignite,
Illuminating dreams through shadowed fright.

As twilight dances with stars to birth,
We find solace in the hush of earth.
Glimmers of hope, they softly call,
In the grip of light, we stand tall.

And though darkness seeks to claim our breath,
The luminous grip conquers death.
With every heartbeat, we feel the spark,
In our veins, a light in the dark.

Through trails of brilliance, we wander wide,
Lost in the wonder, we take the ride.
The grasp of light warms every soul,
Binding us all in its gentle whole.

Enchantment in the Grip of Twilight's Hand

Twilight seeps into the dreaming sky,
Where shadows stretch, and whispers lie.
In the soft grip of dusk's embrace,
Magic dances with ethereal grace.

The stars awaken, sparkling bright,
Glimmers of hope in the cloak of night.
With each heartbeat, the world slows down,
In the twilight, wear no frown.

A lullaby sung by crickets strong,
As time drifts on, the night grows long.
In twilight's hand, we find the spell,
That whispers secrets and bids us dwell.

The brush of night paints dreams so wide,
As we surrender to the tide.
Embraced by shadows, our spirits rise,
In the grip of twilight, hope never dies.

So let us waltz 'neath the silver gleam,
In the twilight's hand, we chase a dream.
With every breath, enchantment flows,
In the soft night air, our magic glows.

Serpentine Shadows and Mythical Light

In the depths of night, shadows creep,
Serpentine forms that twist and leap.
They weave through realms both near and far,
Beneath each whisper, a hidden star.

The dance of light in the darkened fold,
Where mysteries hide, and tales are told.
Mythical creatures in silence glide,
In shadows deep, where dreams abide.

With heartbeats racing, we chase the glow,
Through twisting paths that ebb and flow.
Each glint and shimmer, a fleeting sight,
In serpentine shadows, we find our light.

The shadows beckon with whispered charms,
Drawing us close with unseen arms.
In the dance of dusk, adventure springs,
From shadowed depths, our spirit sings.

So take my hand, let's wander wide,
Through shadows and light, let our hearts bide.
In every turn, enchantments wake,
In serpentine shadows, we shall not break.

Tales of the Feathered Shadows

In twilight's grasp, the whispers call,
Soft secrets danced in shadow's thrall.
Feathers drift like memories lost,
Beneath the stars, they count the cost.

A flicker here, a flutter there,
Echoes linger in the air.
Dreams take flight on gentle wings,
As midnight's tune, the starlight sings.

Oft tales are spun in silver thread,
Of shadowed realms where hopes are fed.
With every beat, the stories blend,
In feathered shadows, they transcend.

An avian voice in the moonlit night,
Guides the heart toward the light.
Through the dark, the spark remains,
In tangled paths, the soul regains.

So listen close, dear dreamer, still,
For tales of shadows always will
Lead the brave, through worlds unseen,
Where feathered whispers weave the keen.

Remnants in the Wake of Legends

Beneath the stars of ancient realm,
Legends linger, dreams overwhelm.
In silent echoes, whispers play,
Their remnants dance at close of day.

Heroes rise with every dawn,
Yet shadows linger, never gone.
With every tale, a truth unfolds,
In weary hearts, their courage molds.

The burdens worn and scars embraced,
In timeless moments, fate is chased.
Echoes of laughter, traces of pain,
In the wake of legends, the heart will gain.

A flicker of hope in darkest strife,
Guides the lost toward new life.
For every legend has a start,
In remnants old, we find the heart.

So gather 'round, and heed the lore,
For in these tales, you'll find the core.
A gentle spark, a guiding flame,
In the wake of legends, we'll rise the same.

The Flight from Dawn's Embrace

As morn awakens with golden light,
The world stirs gently, shy from night.
Yet shadows linger, dreams take flight,
From dawn's embrace, to starry height.

The sky ablaze with colors bold,
Whispers of secrets yet untold.
A dance of clouds, a fleeting kiss,
In every breath, a moment's bliss.

With each heartbeat, horizons stretch,
We chase the dawn, our spirits etch.
Through valleys deep, and mountains high,
In search of wings, we long to fly.

Yet who can say where dreams may lead,
In every heart, a hidden seed.
In flight from dawn, we seek the skies,
Unraveled threads, our spirits rise.

So cherish moments, fleeting, rare,
As dawn's embrace begins to flare.
For every flight from light's sweet grace,
Leads us to lands we long to face.

Stolen Moments in a Mythical Realm

In whispers soft, where shadows dwell,
We find the place where magic swells.
Stolen moments, fleeting, bright,
In mythical realms, they dance with light.

With every step upon the ground,
Dreams entwined, in silence found.
A tapestry of stars above,
In stolen moments, we learn to love.

Through winding paths and hidden doors,
The heart discovers ancient shores.
Where time stands still, and wishes soar,
In mythical realms, forevermore.

The flicker of hope in twilight's haze,
Beckons softly through the maze.
To embrace the dreams we hold so dear,
In stolen moments, we conquer fear.

So close your eyes and take a chance,
In the realm of dreams, we learn to dance.
For in those moments, pure and grand,
Myth meets heart, in magic's hand.

Shadows Fall Where Legends Rest

In twilight's hush, the shadows creep,
Where ancient tales in silence sleep.
The echoes of the past resound,
In hallowed ground where dreams are found.

The moonlit path, a silver thread,
Through whispered winds and tales long dead.
With every breeze, a story told,
Of brave hearts worn and spirits bold.

In cloaks of night, they walk again,
The heroes lost, the noble men.
Their laughter dances on the air,
A haunting tune, both bright and rare.

For in this place, the stars align,
Where legends rest, and hearts entwine.
In shadows deep, the magic stays,
A testament to ancient ways.

So linger on this sacred night,
And feel the pulse of purest light.
For in the dark, where echoes call,
We find the strength of legends all.

Wings of Destiny in Dusk's Embrace

As daylight fades, the sky ignites,
With colors bold, in wondrous sights.
The whispers rise on feathered wings,
A symphony of dreams that sings.

In dusky hues, the world transforms,
As destiny in silence swarms.
With every beat, a tale unfolds,
Of journeys vast and glories bold.

The twilight dances, shadows sway,
In every heart, a choice to play.
Beneath the stars, our fears erase,
And find our strength in night's embrace.

With courage flown on whispered breeze,
Our spirits soar, our minds at ease.
In dusk's sweet glow, we take to flight,
For destiny awaits us bright.

Together, we will face the dark,
Embracing all, igniting spark.
With wings of hope, we shall ascend,
In dusk's warm hug, until the end.

The Forgotten Whispers of Feathered Heroes

In ancient woods where silence reigns,
The whispers of the brave remain.
A feather's touch, a secret passed,
Through time and space, forever cast.

The leaves will tell of soaring heights,
Of heroes lost in fateful flights.
Each rustling branch, a voice of old,
A tale of courage, fierce and bold.

Beneath the boughs, where shadows dwell,
The stories weave a potent spell.
With every gust, the past awakes,
In hallowed ground, the silence breaks.

Their valor sings on whispered winds,
Invisible threads where fate begins.
The feathered brave, so long unseen,
Still hold the earth's most sacred glean.

So listen close, as night descends,
For every breeze, a story lends.
The heroes' echoes shall not wane,
In whispered woods, their power reigns.

Echoes of the Onyx Requiem

In shadows deep, a requiem stirs,
An ode to those, the night confers.
With onyx tones, the silence weaves,
A tapestry of loss that grieves.

The nightingale sings of hearts once bold,
In melodies of stories told.
In hushed tones, their legend flows,
As night wraps gently, silence grows.

From darkened skies, the starlight gleams,
While shadows dance in midnight dreams.
The solemn vows, a whispered plea,
In every note, the spirits free.

Each sigh of wind, a memory's flight,
A shattered soul, a spark of light.
In reverence to those who've gone,
The echoes linger, ever drawn.

So raise your voice, let silence break,
For in this night, their hearts awake.
In onyx hues, their stories blend,
An endless verse that shall not end.

The Dance of Claws and Stars

Beneath the moonlight's silver glow,
The creatures stir, their shadows flow.
With claws that gleam like sharpened steel,
They dance in dreams, their glories reveal.

In whispers soft, the night does sing,
Of ancient tales and splendid wings.
Each paw a brush on canvased night,
As stars look down, a marvel bright.

Around the fire, stories bloom,
Of battles fierce and echoes' gloom.
With laughter ringing through the air,
The woodland creatures shed their care.

The clock ticks by, yet time stands still,
As whispers weave with magic's will.
In this proud grove, they twist and turn,
For every heart holds a lantern's burn.

So join the dance beneath the skies,
Where every leap, a spirit flies.
With claws and stars entwined as one,
The night persists until it's done.

Beneath the Echoing Wings of Time

Beneath the sky, where secrets dwell,
The echoes call, a distant bell.
In shadows cast by ancient trees,
The whispers ride upon the breeze.

A gentle hand of fate appears,
It weaves through dreams, it stirs our fears.
Each tick of clock, a story unfolds,
In twilight's grasp, the past beholds.

Wings whisper low, in silent flight,
They trace the paths of day and night.
Each feathered tale, both soft and bold,
Leaves imprints on the hearts of old.

Through time's embrace, we chase our quest,
With every breath, we seek the best.
In fleeting moments, we shall find,
The strength of love, the ties that bind.

So heed the call of moments spent,
Beneath the heavens, soft and gentle bent.
For in the dance of wings and time,
Our souls entwine in rhythmic rhyme.

When Darkness Weaves Its Threads

When darkness falls, and shadows creep,
The world turns still, the night does weep.
In corners deep, the secrets hide,
While phantoms weave their velvet tide.

Amidst the silence, echoes roar,
Of tales once told, now lost to lore.
With threads unseen, the weaver spins,
A fabric rich with tales of sins.

The moon's pale light, a stolen glance,
Illuminates the specter's dance.
In every thread, there lies a tale,
Of lonely hearts that sought to sail.

Yet through the darkness, hope does rise,
Like dawn's embrace, brightening lies.
For every thread that's drawn in fright,
A spark of courage brings forth light.

So when the night begins to swell,
Remember well, each woven spell.
For in the dark, the magic sways,
With every breath, it gently plays.

Whispers of Fate Amidst Feathered Might

In realms where whispers seize the light,
The feathered might takes graceful flight.
With every flap, a promise soars,
A tale unfolds behind closed doors.

Beneath the sun, where shadows blend,
The fates entangle, twist and bend.
With wings unfurled, the spirits gleam,
They ride the winds, alive with dream.

The whispers sing of lives unknown,
Of hearts that bare their seeds and bone.
And every cry, a thread is spun,
A tapestry of dusk and sun.

Through tempest storms and tranquil skies,
The echoes linger, never die.
In every feather, stories loom,
Of love and loss, of pain and bloom.

So heed the whispers of the night,
For fate's own song brings visions bright.
Amidst the feathered might they find,
A binding truth, forever kind.

Beneath the Weight of Gilded Dreams

In chambers where the shadows churn,
The gilded echoes quietly yearn.
Whispers cling to the velvet air,
Amidst illusions, the heart lays bare.

Chasing visions that softly gleam,
A dance ensnares the fleeting dream.
Under starlit secrets, we weave,
What we treasure, we also grieve.

Each hope a fragile strand of light,
Caught in a tapestry of night.
With every breath, the layers peel,
Revealing truths we start to feel.

But breaths can fade in golden glow,
As worries bloom, and shadows grow.
Yet underneath, a spark remains,
A light that strengthens through the chains.

So let us gather those dreams we hold,
Transform the shadows into gold.
For in the weight of what it's worth,
We find our purpose here on Earth.

A Dance with Myth in Midnight's Embrace

Beneath the moon's enchanted gaze,
Myth and magic start to blaze.
Figures twirl in cosmic flight,
Whispers vibrant in the night.

Footsteps echo, rhythms slow,
Fables twined in silver glow.
From ancient tales, the spirits call,
In twilight's arms, we sway and fall.

With mysteries wrapped in stardust fine,
We grasp the threads that intertwine.
Legends breathe, take shape anew,
As we dance in dreams, like morning dew.

Yet the clock's steady tick reminds,
Of fleeting moments life unwinds.
Still, in our hearts, the stories stay,
Guiding us through night and day.

In midnight's hold, we twirl as one,
Beneath the canopy of the sun.
Embracing myth till dawn's embrace,
Forever lost in time and space.

The Bonds of Ancient Talons

High above in the silvered skies,
Ancient talons deftly rise.
With every flap, the echoes sing,
Of timeless bonds and what they bring.

The whispers of the winds so brave,
Journeying forth across the wave.
Nestled close in shadows' fold,
The stories waiting to be told.

With each alliance forged in flight,
A testament to shared delight.
From sharpest beak to claw's embrace,
In unity, they find their place.

Through storm and strife, they lift and soar,
The ancient dance forevermore.
In shared endeavors, hearts align,
Creating legacies divine.

So let us honor those who strive,
To keep the bonds of dreams alive.
For in the skies where talons mate,
We find our strength to navigate.

Shadows of the Celestial Keeper

In twilight's cloak, the keeper waits,
Where shadows weave through heaven's gates.
Stars ignite the velvet night,
Guardians veiled in mystic light.

With each whisper from the moon,
The universe sings a somber tune.
Time flows softly through the dark,
As celestial giants leave their mark.

In dreams, the keeper's gaze we seek,
For guidance when the heart feels weak.
Their wisdom lingers, pure and deep,
A promise made, a vow to keep.

The whispers of the void invite,
Embracing all within their sight.
In every shadow, truth is found,
A sanctuary, safe and sound.

So fear not the darkness that surrounds,
For in its arms, true hope abounds.
The celestial keeper holds the key,
Unlocking light for you and me.

Bound by Night's Winged Guardians

In shadows deep, the whispers call,
The guardians rise, both fierce and small.
With wings that shimmer, they guard the night,
In sacred secrets, they take their flight.

Beneath the moon, a silent pact,
They weave the tales of the brave intact.
With every flutter, dreams take flight,
In realms unseen, they chase the light.

The forest stirs with magic's breath,
In twilight's veil, they dance with death.
For where they roam, the lost are found,
In midnight's grace, their hearts resound.

A flicker here, a flutter there,
With eyes like stars, they pierce the air.
In harmony they sing their song,
As timeless threads pull fate along.

So heed the call of night's decree,
Bound by the stars, the brave roam free.
In guardians' wings, our spirits soar,
For with their watch, we fear no more.

Twilight's Grip on the Brave and Bold

In twilight's grip, the brave convene,
With hearts ablaze, they chase the unseen.
The world transformed by softening light,
Stirs courage anew, ignites the night.

With whispered hopes, they venture forth,
In shadows cast, they measure worth.
Each step a promise, each breath a vow,
To face the unknown, unyielding now.

The stars above, like watchful eyes,
Guide every move, their ancient ties.
In unity bound, they march as one,
Through dusk's embrace, till night is done.

The echoes fade, yet still they fight,
To carve their names in the fabric of night.
For heroes rise where darkness bleeds,
With every heartbeat, adventure leads.

So lift your gaze to the heavens wide,
Embrace the magic where dreams abide.
In twilight's grip, the brave and bold,
Shall weave their tales for futures untold.

The Pact of Shadowed Feathers

In forests deep, where silence reigns,
The pact was forged 'neath silvered veins.
With shadowed feathers, the owls took flight,
Guardians of secrets through the velvet night.

A whispered oath, a bond so true,
They gather strength, old and new.
In hues of twilight, they weave their song,
With wisdom shared, to guide the strong.

Each feather dropped, a tale unfurls,
In hidden realms where magic swirls.
Through tempest winds and gentle sighs,
In every rustle, their legacy lies.

So trust the wings that grace the gloom,
For in their clasp, there's light from doom.
In moonlit whispers, the pact shall stand,
As shadows dance, hand in hand.

With each new dawn, the feathers glide,
In harmony, they choose to bide.
Together forever, in night's embrace,
They carry forth the sacred trace.

Silence in the Vale of Myth

In the vale where whispers fade away,
Lies the heart of myths, where dreams hold sway.
Silence lingers, heavy and deep,
Guarding the secrets that legends keep.

Upon the breeze, lost tales drift near,
In shadows long, the past appears.
With every breath, the echoes rise,
Crafting a tapestry of lullabies.

The moonlight spills like silver lace,
Illuminating the enchanted space.
In stillness, truths begin to twine,
Binding the threads of the divine.

Among the trees, ancient spirits roam,
In silence, they whisper, calling us home.
Their voices dance on the misty air,
In the vale of myth, souls laid bare.

So tread with care, in shadows deep,
For the vale holds secrets, still and steep.
With hearts attuned to the silent breath,
We'll find our way beyond time and death.

A Dreamers' Call to Winged Lore

In twilight's hush, the whispers sigh,
A dreamer stirs beneath the sky.
With wings of hope, the night unfolds,
A tale of magic yet untold.

The stars ignite a silver trail,
As shadows dance on night's soft veil.
From distant realms where wonders gleam,
The dreamers waltz within their dream.

In whispered winds, the secrets weave,
Of flights above, where none believe.
A beckoning from realms afar,
To find their truth beneath the stars.

Each glance towards the heavens flows,
With promise wrapped in moonlit prose.
Their wings unfurl, a soft embrace,
A journey sought in boundless space.

Through realms of dusk, their spirits rise,
To touch the ever-changing skies.
In every heart, the dreamers call,
To weave their fate, to soar, to fall.

Shadows Unfurled in Mythic Deluge

In ancient woods, where shadows creep,
The tales of yore in silence seep.
A deluge deep of lore unfolds,
As whispered secrets dare be told.

The moonlit paths where echoes tread,
Beneath the boughs where myths are bred.
With every rustle, ghosts awake,
In twilight's grasp, their whispers quake.

The shadows weave a tapestry,
Of lost enchantments, wild and free.
In every hush, the past reborn,
As stars ignite the misty morn.

They speak of battles, brave and bold,
Of heroes lost and legends old.
As echoes fade in twilight's breath,
The stories linger, dance with death.

In depths unknown, the night shall spill,
The mystic lore, the ancient thrill.
For shadows, dark, entwine our fate,
In mythos drawn from time's own gate.

The Sanctuary of Feathered Trust

In hidden glades, where softness dwells,
The air is rich with untold spells.
A sanctuary, warm and bright,
Where feathered friends take graceful flight.

Among the leaves, the whispering breeze,
Carries secrets home, with tender ease.
Guardians of dreams, they gather near,
In melodies only hearts can hear.

The trees embrace their wings of gold,
With every flutter, tales unfold.
In circles drawn by laughter sweet,
A trust is sown where spirits meet.

From heights above, they soar and glide,
In unity, they turn the tide.
A bond unbroken, strong and true,
In every heart, their spirit grew.

So let us dance beneath their grace,
In this safe haven, a warm space.
Together, with the winged delight,
We find our home in shared pure light.

The Lament of the Winged Ancients

Where skies once danced with vibrant hues,
The ancients call in solemn blues.
Their voices rise like tempest's song,
A haunting echo, deep and long.

In twilight's grip, their shadows blend,
With whispers soft that never end.
Through crags and cliffs, their stories weep,
Of journeys taken, lost in sleep.

The winds do carry their soft sighs,
As aching hearts and freedom flies.
In every flutter, memories swell,
Of realms forsaken, tales to tell.

The stars bear witness to their flight,
As night enfolds the weary light.
A lament etched in silence clear,
Of all they cherished, once held dear.

Yet through the sorrow, hope does rise,
A promise born beyond the skies.
For in the twilight's deep embrace,
The winged ancients find their place.

Heartstrings Tied in Celestial Flight

In the realm where wishes soar,
Hearts weave tales, forevermore.
Stars above in velvet night,
Guide the dreams that take their flight.

Whispers float on moonlit beams,
Tugging at our secret schemes.
Each heartbeat syncs with the sky,
As hopes and stardust gently lie.

Through the mist of dreams we glide,
With every wish, a cosmic tide.
Celestial strings pull us near,
Enfolding us in love's own sphere.

Dancing through the cosmic glow,
Where paths unfold and futures flow.
Together, hearts begin to weave,
A tapestry of what we believe.

In this world where starlight gleams,
We chase the pulse of our wild dreams.
Heartstrings tied, forever bright,
In the magic of the night.

The Tangle of Stars and Dreams

In the quiet folds of dusk,
Dreams entwined in silken husk.
Stars like jewels in the sky,
Whisper secrets as they fly.

A tapestry of dark and light,
Dancing shadows, igniting sight.
The cosmos hums an ancient tune,
Revealing paths to hidden moons.

Each glance reveals a story spun,
Where the galaxies once begun.
A cosmic tangle, bright and bold,
Where wishes simmer, close yet cold.

Through the labyrinth of night we roam,
Chasing dreams that feel like home.
Each heartbeat syncs with stardust sway,
Guiding us along the way.

Connected by this mystic thread,
We dance where once the stars have led.
In the tangle, we find our breath,
In dreams alive, no trace of death.

An Ode to the Shaded Conceit

In shadows cast by dreams unspoken,
Lies a truth that feels like token.
Veils of night hold countless lies,
Where the shaded heart denies.

An ode is sung to what we wear,
The masks we show, the souls laid bare.
In every glance, a silent plea,
Beneath the shades, we long to be.

Her whispers float on breezes warm,
Twisting thoughts, a perfect charm.
In darkness, we create our art,
Yet hide the tender, aching heart.

As shadows dance, we find our way,
In shaded arcs of night and day.
Each pose, a fleeting, fragile scheme,
Yet in the dusk, we dare to dream.

In this conceit of light and dark,
We find the echo of our spark.
A journey led by heart's decree,
In shaded realms, we seek to be.

In the Embrace of Twilight's Grip

In twilight's soft and gentle clutch,
The world around, a sacred hush.
Colors blend in Painter's dream,
As night descends, our spirits beam.

Here, the stars take fragile flight,
Weaving magic through the night.
With each fading beam of gold,
Stories whispered, secrets told.

In this embrace, we find our rest,
Heartbeats syncing, souls confessed.
The moonlight drapes our hopes anew,
In twilight's arms, we're born to two.

With shadows creeping o'er the land,
We join the dance, hand in hand.
Through silence deep, we hear the call,
In twilight's grip, we find our all.

As day surrenders to the night,
We weave our dreams in silver light.
In twilight's hush, our hearts ignite,
Together, we embrace the night.

When Shadows Conspire Among the Stars

In twilight's hush, the whispers weave,
A dance of fate, no hearts deceive.
Beneath the moon, the shadows creep,
Secrets shared in silence deep.

The cosmos hums a tune of old,
In quiet realms, where tales unfold.
Stars align in silent pact,
A woven thread, by night enacted.

With every flicker, magic glows,
In the darkness, a world bestows.
Through stardust paths, the wanderers tread,
With dreams of light, and hopes unsaid.

As shadows stretch, the night reveals,
The stories held, the fate it seals.
From every corner, glimmers shine,
In this vast sky, all souls entwine.

So linger long, let quiet reign,
Embrace the stars, release the pain.
For in the void, where dreams conspire,
We find our hearts, and reignite the fire.

Reverence Held in Grasped Talons

Upon the cliff, where eagles soar,
The winds sing songs of ancient lore.
With talons sharp, they clutch the sky,
In every flight, their spirits high.

The mountains bow to regal grace,
As shadows dance, they find their place.
A symphony of feathers bright,
Awakens dreams in morning light.

In silent vigil, they survey all,
Bold sentinels, neither proud nor small.
With every beat of wings they carve,
A trail of strength that none could starve.

They circle high, through azure streams,
And guard the land of whispered dreams.
With reverence held in grasped talons,
They chart the skies, they weave the balance.

Return they must, as dusk descends,
To crags and nests where twilight blends.
In their embrace, the world finds peace,
A heavenly dance that will not cease.

The Loom of Night in Mythic Ornament

In shadows cast, the loom is spun,
Threads of silver, no day begun.
The stars emerge in twilight's clutch,
Each gleaming orb, a tender touch.

Through woven tales, the night unfolds,
Histories wrapped in whispers told.
In silken strands, the dreams ignite,
A tapestry of pure delight.

With every stitch, a spell to bind,
Moments captured, you will find.
Mythic creatures in quiet grace,
Dance to rhythms lost in space.

As midnight's heart begins to swell,
In every corner, secrets dwell.
The loom of night, with magic laced,
Creates a world, forever embraced.

In this dark realm, where dreams hold sway,
The threads of hope, a bright array.
So wander forth, embrace the night,
In its deep grasp, find your light.

Visions in the Glare of Feathered Gaze

In rustling leaves, a gaze appears,
With knowing eyes that drown in fears.
Each feathered stroke, a story shared,
In every glance, a heart laid bare.

Beneath the boughs, the whispers rise,
Entwined in magic, dreams disguise.
The world unfolds in silent truth,
Awakening the heart of youth.

Through veils of dusk, the vision calls,
While echoes dance in hidden halls.
A feathered glance, a potion brewed,
In twilight's grip, the path renewed.

So watch the skies for tales untold,
In every rustle, the brave and bold.
In night's embrace, let visions blaze,
Illuminated by the feathered gaze.

With every flutter, secrets wake,
In the silence, the shadows break.
For in their eyes, adventure twines,
In the glare of night, our fate aligns.

.

www.ingramcontent.com/pod-product-compliance
Ingram Content Group UK Ltd.
Pitfield, Milton Keynes, MK11 3LW, UK
UKHW021435220125
4239UKWH00039B/690

9 781805 647423